W9-BDK-967

Spin it Figure Skating

SPORTS STARTERS

Paul Challen

🌳 Crabtree Publishing Company

www.crabtreebooks.com

SPORTS STARTERS

Created by Bobbie Kalman

Author
Paul Challen

Project coordinator
Kathy Middleton

Editors
Molly Aloian
Rachel Stuckey

Photo research
Melissa McClellan

Design
Tibor Choleva
Melissa McClellan

Production coordinator
Ken Wright

Prepress technician
Ken Wright

Illustrations
Leif Peng: page 11

Photographs
Skate Canada Archives: pages 3, 4, 7, 9, 12, 14,
    15, 17, 18, 20, 22, 26, 28
Shutterstock.com: cover and back cover; pages 1, 5 (top), 6, 16, 19,
    24, 25, 31 (bottom), 31 (middle),
Dreamstime.com: pages 5 (bottom), 7, 8, 13, 21, 23, 27, 29
iStockphoto.com: page 31 (top)

Special thanks to
Emery Leger of Skate Canada and Skate Canada

Created for Crabtree Publishing by Silver Dot Publishers

Library and Archives Canada Cataloguing in Publication

Challen, Paul, 1967-
    Spin it figure skating / Paul Challen.

(Sports starters)
Includes index.
ISBN 978-0-7787-3146-7 (bound).--ISBN 978-0-7787-3178-8 (pbk.)

    1. Figure skating--Juvenile literature. I. Title. II. Series: Sports
starters (St. Catharines, Ont.)

GV850.4.C43 2010   j796.91'2   C2009-906939-3

Library of Congress Cataloging-in-Publication Data

Challen, Paul C. (Paul Clarence), 1967-
 Spin it figure skating / Paul Challen.
     p. cm. -- (Sports starters)
 Includes index.
 ISBN 978-0-7787-3178-8 (pbk. : alk. paper) -- ISBN 978-0-7787-3146-7
(reinforced library binding : alk. paper)
 1. Figure skating--Juvenile literature. I. Title.

GV850.4.C47 2010
796.91'2--dc22

                                        2009048052

Crabtree Publishing Company

Printed in the U.S.A./122009/CG20091120

www.crabtreebooks.com   1-800-387-7650

Published in Canada
Crabtree Publishing
616 Welland Ave.
St. Catharines, Ontario
L2M 5V6

Published in the United States
Crabtree Publishing
PMB 59051
350 Fifth Ave., 59th Floor
New York, NY 10118

Published in the United Kingdom
Crabtree Publishing
Maritime House
Basin Road North, Hove
BN411 1WR

Published in Australia
Crabtree Publishing
386 Mt. Alexander Rd.
Ascot Vale (Melbourne)
VIC 3032

Contents

What is figure skating?   4

Gearing up   6

Keeping score   8

Inside the arena   10

Together now!   12

Jump!   14

Airborne   16

Lift it!   18

Spin zone   20

Turning it on   22

Pump up the volume!   24

The competitive scene   26

Just for show   28

Hit the ice!   30

Glossary and Index   32

What is figure skating?

Figure skating is a sport that takes place on ice. Skaters glide around the ice and do difficult moves including **spins** and **jumps**. When figure skating is done by one person it is called **individual figure skating**. When two skaters perform together, it is called **pair figure skating** and **ice dancing**.

An individual skater combines concentration with skill, and performs on the ice surface alone.

4

Fun and fitness

Figure skating can be done in competition against other skaters. But it is also a great way to have fun and stay in shape. Practicing figure skating develops strength and flexibility.

Figure skating takes a lot of practice.

Skaters test their skills in competition.

5

Gearing up

Figure skaters wear special skates. The skates have blades with "teeth" at the end called **toe picks**. The toe picks help skaters' blades dig into the ice. This allows skaters to perform many difficult moves. When they are not on the ice, figure skaters protect the blades on their skates with skate guards.

Figure skates have blades that are different from regular skates.

What to wear

Figure skaters usually wear comfortable clothing that is snug. In competition, skaters wear colorful outfits. In pair and ice dancing competitions, partners often have matching outfits.

Costumes add color to competitive skating.

Keeping score

In a figure skating competition, **officials**, or judges, watch the skaters. Each skater or pair completes a series of moves called a **routine**. When an individual or pair is finished skating, the officials give the routine a **score**. This score is based on how well a skater or pair performs the routine and how many mistakes it contains. The more mistakes, the lower the score!

Falls and other mistakes lower a skater's score.

These officials are watching a routine at a competition.

Here comes the official!

Figure skating officials are people who know the sport very well. Many of them are or were skaters themselves. They know what to look for in a routine, such as **grace**, smooth **turns**, and speed. Officials understand that the moves can be very difficult.

Inside the arena

At a skating competition, there is a lot going on. Fans gather to watch the skaters. Officials sit in a special area to watch the action. Some skaters practice their routines in a warm-up area. Other skaters compete on the main ice surface.

Hey coach!

One of the most important people at the arena is the **coach**. A figure skating coach helps skaters practice their routines and encourages them during competitions. They also teach them how to perform moves safely.

A skating arena has an area for officials, a place for fans, a warm-up area, and the ice surface itself.

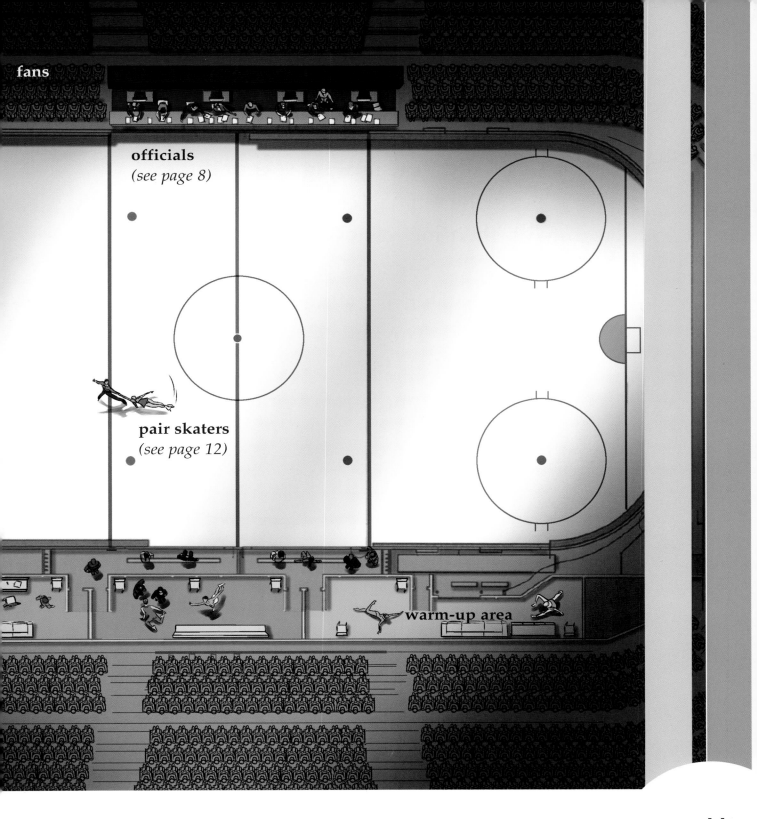

fans

officials
(see page 8)

pair skaters
(see page 12)

warm-up area

Together now!

Pair figure skating is very difficult. Partners have to cooperate with one another to do their moves together at the same speed. Pairs are always made up of one male skater and one female skater. They perform moves including **lifts** and spins. The male skater always lifts the female skater. Pair figure skating requires strength, timing, balance, and a lot of practice.

In pair figure skating, skaters often perform moves at angles that seem impossible!

A question of trust

It is very important that partners in pair figure skating trust one another. After all, throwing someone into the air and spinning them around is not easy. As you fly through the air, it is good to know there will be someone to catch you!

Pair skaters communicate to get their timing just right.

Jump!

Jumps are a big part of figure skating routines. In a jump, a skater leaps and then spins around in the air. But that is not all. The skater also has to land without stumbling or falling. In pair skating, the male partner throws the female partner into the air to do spins.

Jumps take strength and concentration.

Practice makes perfect

Jumps might look easy, but they require a lot of practice. Skaters work for many hours with coaches to learn jumps. When a skater is learning a new jump, coaches will sometimes use ropes and cables to help him or her to fly through the air safely. Skaters often practice landing on mats in a gym before trying the jump on ice.

Jumpers try to land without stumbling or falling.

Airborne

There are different kinds of jumps that skaters perform. In a **toe jump**, a skater takes off by launching from the toe pick of one skate. In an **edge jump**, the skater uses the edge of one skate for takeoff. No matter what kind of jump a skater tries, he or she is looking to get as much height above the ice as possible.

All jumps start with a strong takeoff.

Spinning it!

When a skater is in the air, he or she can also try a number of spinning moves. These are named for how many times the skater spins around. In a **single jump**, the skater spins around once. In a **double jump**, he or she spins twice. Just imagine how hard it is to do a triple jump!

It takes great body control to spin.

Lift it!

In pair skating, partners perform lifts. In a lift, the male partner lifts the female partner overhead. The female partner performs moves while high above the ice. The male partner sometimes performs single or double **rotations** on the ice as he holds his partner in the air.

One-armed lifts are very difficult.

The lifted skater can use a number of positions to win points with officials.

Timing it

Lifts require a lot of strength, balance, and skating skill. In competition, partners have to hold the lifted position for at least three seconds for it to count in their final score.

Spin zone

One of the most exciting parts of any figure skating routine is the spin. To do a spin, a skater pushes on the part of the skate blade that is just behind the toe pick and forces his or her body to spin around. It takes a lot of strength to do a spin on the ice and in the air.

Flexibility is key for most spins.

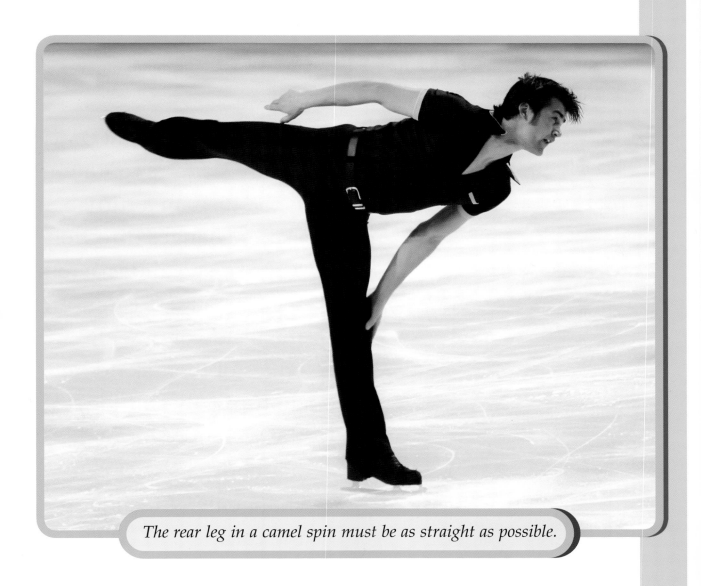

The rear leg in a camel spin must be as straight as possible.

Name game

Different figure skating spins have different names.
For example, in a **camel spin**, a skater keeps one skate
on the ice, while bending over and sticking his or her
other leg straight out behind his or her body.

Turning it on

Another important part of any skater's routine is the turn. In a turn, a skater changes direction as he or she glides across the ice. Skaters can use the inside or outside edges of their skates to do turns. By shifting the weight of his or her body, a skater can change the direction of the turn.

Pairs must time their turns perfectly.

The eagle has landed

One common move in figure skating is the **spread eagle**. In this move, the skater points both skates outward, with the heels pointed at one another. He or she turns on the inside or outside edge of the blades, often with arms outstretched. In this position, the skater resembles an eagle with its wings spread!

Turns depend on control of the skate edges.

Pump up the volume!

Figure skating routines are set to music. That means that parts of the routine match with parts of the music. Fast spins and jumps go best with fast music. Graceful turns match up best with slow music. Both individual and pair skating use music.

Music and costumes get the crowd excited.

Ice dancing is an Olympic sport.

Dance, dance, dance

Ice dancing is a type of figure skating. Ice dancers take moves from ballet and other types of dance and build them into their routines. Music is very important in this style of figure skating.

The competitive scene

Figure skating competitions take place all over the world. The **International Skating Union (ISU)** makes sure that officials and skaters follow the rules of the sport. Every year, the ISU holds the World Figure Skating Championships. Every four years, the Winter Olympic Games also has a figure skating competition. Figure skating is one of the most popular sports in the Winter Olympics, with both individual and pair events attracting huge crowds.

Canadians Jamie Sale and David Pelletier are masters of pair competition.

The greats of the sport

Some great skaters of the past include pair stars Jamie Sale and David Pelletier of Canada; Kristi Yamaguchi, Dorothy Hamill, Peggy Fleming, and Scott Hamilton of the USA; and pair team Yelena Berezhnaya and Anton Sikharulidze of Russia. Today's stars include the 2009 men's world champion Evan Lysacek of the USA and Kim Yu-Na of South Korea, the women's champion.

Kim Yu-Na of South Korea is the 2009 women's world champion.

Just for show

Figure skating **exhibitions** also attract a lot of fans. Exhibitions are not competitions. Instead, skaters hit the ice in colorful costumes, using their best moves to entertain the crowd, just for the fun of it. Often, skaters dress up as popular characters from movies and television shows to thrill the crowd.

Costumes are a big part of a skating exhibition.

Exhibitions often feature many skaters on the ice at once.

Hit the ice!

Figure skating is a great way to stay in shape. It builds strong muscles, flexibility, and coordination. Learning to do some of the complicated moves in figure skating also requires a lot of concentration and determination.

Of course, you can practice figure skating moves on any ice surface, but it is a good idea to have a grown-up around for safety—and to give you some pointers. If you are interested in learning more about figure skating, local figure skating clubs are great places to practice and compete.

Wherever there is ice, there is figure skating!

Glossary

Note: Boldfaced words that are defined in the text may not appear in the glossary.

exhibition A non-competitive skating event where skaters entertain the crowd

grace The ability to move smoothly and easily

ice dancing A form of figure skating that uses moves from ballet and other forms of dance

individual figure skating Figure skating done by a single person

jump An important figure skating move that happens when a skater launches him or herself into the air

lift A move in pair figure skating when one partner lifts the other high overhead

official The person who determines a skater's score in competition

pair figure skating Figure skating done by two partners who work together to perform moves

rotation One complete turn of the body in a figure skating spin or jump

routine A combination of figure skating moves

score In competition, a number given to a routine based on how well it was performed by a skater or pair

spin An important figure skating move that happens when a skater rotates either on the ice or above it in a jump

toe picks Sharp points at the end of a figure skate's blade that help a skater dig into the ice

turn A move that a skater uses to change direction on the ice

Index

camel spin 21

coach 10, 15

costumes 7, 24, 28

double jump 17

edge jump 16

exhibitions 28, 29

fitness 5, 30

ice dancing 4, 25

individual figure skating 4

International Skating
   Union (ISU) 26

jump 4, 14-15, 16, 24

lift 12, 18-19

music 24

officials 8-9, 10-11, 19, 26

pair figure skating 4, 12-13

routine 8-9, 10, 14, 20, 22,
   24-25

score 8-9, 19

single jump 17

skates 6

spin 4, 12, 13, 14, 17, 20-21, 24

spread eagle 23

toe jump 16

toe pick 6, 16, 20

triple jump 17

turn 9, 22, 24